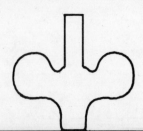

PRESSING FLOWERS AND LEAVES

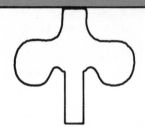
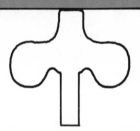

WARREN FARNWORTH

ILLUSTRATED BY WARREN FARNWORTH AND ELIZABETH HAINES

A CHATTO ACTIVITY BOOK

CHATTO AND WINDUS

Published by Chatto and Windus Ltd.
42 William IV Street, London WC2

Clarke, Irwin and Co. Ltd., Toronto

© Warren Farnworth 1973

ISBN 0 7011 5037 8

Printed in Great Britain by
Martin's of Berwick

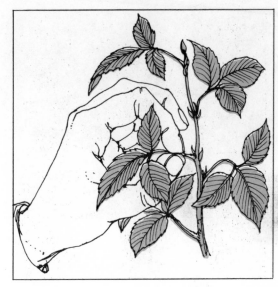

CONTENTS

INTRODUCTION

Have you ever turned the pages of an old book and found a pressed flower, faded and dry? Who could have put it there, and why?

Could it have been a young girl who picked it and pressed it to remind her of a happy day in the country? Or a botanist who picked it for his collection? Or a bride, to remind her of her wedding day? Who knows? People have pressed flowers for all kinds of reasons.

Queen Victoria, we are told, pressed them to remind her of her dead husband: '*the inconsolable Queen started an album of pressed flowers, the early pages of which have flowers which lay on the Prince's bed during his last illness; also of leaves from the wreath given by the Princesses.*' Others

because they thought it a useful hobby, very suitable for young Victorian ladies with little else to do.

But before long, people found it much more artistic to arrange their dried flowers into a picture, and to add a carefully chosen poem. In Queen Victoria's day, it became very fashionable. Everybody began to do it. Some made Valentine cards to send to their friends. Others made pictures to hang on the wall. And some made pressed flower pictures to sell at the village fête, giving the money to a poor children's home, or using it to buy warm blankets to send to soldiers fighting overseas.

All that was a long time ago. Now, pressed flower pictures are seldom seen. But why not?

Perhaps this is the time to start again, and here's what to do . . .

COLLECTING LEAVES AND FLOWERS

Most kinds of leaves and flowers are suitable for pressing, but some are better than others. With practice you will soon become quite expert in knowing what to pick and what not to pick.

To begin with, pick the kinds of leaves and flowers which can easily be pressed flat. A sycamore leaf would be all right, but not the leaf and the twig together, for the twig would be much too hard and thick to press. Very large leaves like dock or rhubarb might cause difficulties because of their size and their thick veins and stems.

Flowers with lots of petals like roses or large Michaelmas daisies can be used if you pick off the petals one by one and press them separately, but would be much too thick to press whole.

The ones you must never pick are those which are dangerous, poisonous, or rare.

Nettles and brambles are a little dangerous because they can sting or scratch. But even more dangerous are the plants which grow in or near water, or in a marsh. The plants themselves may be harmless enough, but not so the place where you find them. However tempting that water-lily might seem, or however colourful the flowers in the marsh, leave them alone.

Poisonous plants are less easy to spot, but beware of those which have shiny red, white or purple berries, and never put strange plants to your lips, or try to eat them.

Last of all, the rare ones. Be especially careful when picking flowers in the country. If the plant is a strange one, leave it alone; a good rule to follow is to pick a plant only when there are lots of the same kind growing nearby. If you are in a National Trust property you must not pick plants at all; and remember that in certain areas it is against the law to uproot well-known flowers like primroses and bluebells.

6

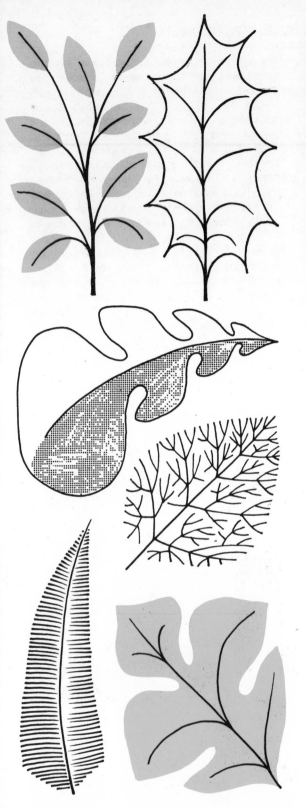

Begin your collection by looking around for some of the very common leaves and flowers which you will find growing in your garden, or near your home. Beech leaves and hawthorn, clover and daisies, dandelions, horse-chestnut, buttercups and ash.

Most of these, and many more, should be very easy to find, and no one will be annoyed if you begin by picking more than you really need.

If you live in a block of flats in a city, and have difficulty finding flowers and leaves, keep a sharp lookout on your way to school, and make a note of the plants and trees growing on any patches of spare ground.

Better still, if you know of an old lady with a large garden full of weeds, offer to weed it for her. She will be glad of your help, and you will be able to add lots of new leaves and flowers to your collection. When later you make your dried flower pictures, weeds will be every bit as useful as the rarest orchid.

As your collection grows, you must begin to think more carefully about what to pick, and what not to pick. Try not to pick too many of one kind of flower or leaf, and make sure that those which you do pick are in good condition.

Collect as many different shapes, sizes and colours of leaves and flowers as you possibly can, not forgetting the many different kinds of grasses, stalks and ferns. If you search carefully, you should be able to find most of the shapes which you see here.

7

HOW TO COLLECT

Always take great care when picking specimens from a living plant. Try not to tug or pull at the plant, and never ever pull it out by the roots just to collect a few flowers or leaves. Gently pinch off the pieces which you want between finger and thumb. If the stem is too strong, cut off the piece with a pair of scissors or a penknife. This way, no harm will come to the plant, and new buds and leaves will grow again, ready for someone else to pick in the future. As soon as a leaf or flower is picked, it begins to die, so you must keep it fresh until it is pressed. If you are picking flowers in your own garden, you can take them back into the house and press them right away, but what do you do if you are on a flower-picking expedition away from home?

1. You can keep your specimens fresh by putting them in a plastic bag, the top held together with an elastic band. This is much easier than having to carry a basket or a jam-jar full of water.

But take care not to let the younger children play with your pickings, and never leave the plastic bags lying about the countryside. Cows and foxes are very inquisitive creatures, and they would be very ill, and might even die, if they ate one of them.

2. You can press your specimens as you pick them by putting them between the pages of a book. Any old book will do, but preferably one which has soft, absorbent pages (not the very shiny kind), and one which you can easily carry about. Who wants to carry an encyclopedia on a country walk?

Better still, you could make your own carrying press. It's quite easy, and you would find it very useful for holidays and trips in the country.

You will need two pieces of plywood about 25 cm by 20 cm, an old leather or plastic belt with a buckle, and about 20 to 30 sheets of paper (newspaper will do), cut to the size of the plywood.

To make it even stronger, you can nail the belt to the plywood covers, and make some kind of carrying handle.

When it's finished, it will look like this.

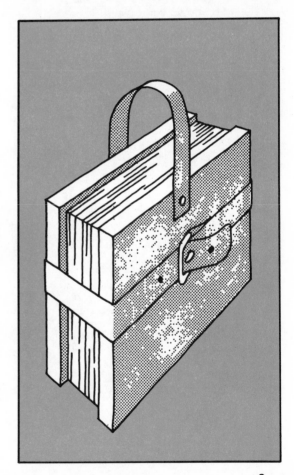

WHEN TO COLLECT

The Time of Day

If you were very professional, you would only pick your leaves and flowers in the afternoon on a bright sunny day. By then, the flowers would be fully open, and the sun would have dried out the morning dew, or the rain which may have fallen during the night. But it isn't always possible to pick your flowers in the afternoon, particularly if you want to collect some specimens on your way to school in the morning, or happen to see something rather special late in the evening; and can you ever be sure of a sunny day? The important thing to remember is to collect only dry specimens. If you really must collect your flowers after a shower of rain, then be sure to dry them off as soon as possible by ironing them between two sheets of paper. (Page 16 shows you how to do this.)

If you don't, the specimen will go mouldy, and be quite useless for making pictures. It might also affect the other dry specimens too. The golden rule is never to press any specimens which are wet — or even just a little damp.

The Time of Year

Spring and summer are best, because then there is so much to choose from; but they aren't the only times. In autumn there are fallen leaves, from green to brightest red, not to mention roses, chrysanthemums, and lots of flowering weeds. And even in winter, when most of the flowers have died, and trees are bare, there is still a lot to find. Tiny snowdrops, violets, primrose and crocus, ferns, grasses, and all the evergreens.

COMMON GRASSES · SCENTLESS MAYWEED · BURNET SAXIFRAGE · HARE-BELL · PANSY · DOG ROSE · BEECH · OAK · ASH · ASTER · WILLOW · DAISY

So pick your flowers and leaves all the year round, and be sure always to have something in your press, ready to be used.

Lastly, a word about colours. Don't be surprised or disappointed if the colours of your specimens change after being dried and pressed. All flowers and leaves do this, although some will take longer to change than others.

Lilac flowers, sweet peas and dahlias, however colourful when first you pick them, will soon turn brown. Most rose petals, except for the very deep red ones, will turn cream. But they can still be very beautiful, especially when you put lots of different kinds of brown leaves and flowers together to make a picture.

Pansies, marigolds, geraniums, primroses, and many of the yellow and orange-coloured flowers will keep their true colour for a long time. Marigolds will stay yellow for about a year, before turning brown. Buttercups will stay yellow for over three years. And best of all, the delphinium will keep its blue for almost ten years.

Other leaves and flowers will produce different colours, depending on when you pick them. Ash leaves picked in the early spring will turn black; beech leaves will be green; whilst in the autumn, both beech and ash will give you reds and browns. Raspberry leaves, whenever you pick them, will be silvery-grey on their underside.

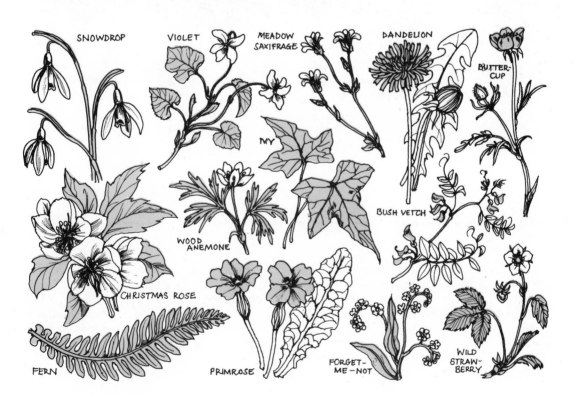

SNOWDROP VIOLET MEADOW SAXIFRAGE DANDELION BUTTER-CUP IVY WOOD ANEMONE BUSH VETCH CHRISTMAS ROSE FERN PRIMROSE FORGET-ME-NOT WILD STRAW-BERRY

DRYING AND PRESSING

Let's suppose that you have just returned from a flower-picking expedition, having collected all kinds of flowers, leaves, ferns and grasses. What do you do next?

1. Find somewhere quiet to work, where you can spread out and examine all the specimens which you have collected. A large kitchen table would do (if your mother isn't too busy), or maybe your bedroom floor. But wherever it is, make sure that it is free from draughts (remember that some of your specimens will be very delicate, and might easily be blown away), and always cover your working space with sheets of newspaper, to keep things clean and tidy.

2. Spread out your specimens for inspection, and sort them out into their different types, shapes, sizes and colours. Small leaves here, large leaves there. Ferns in this corner, flower-heads in that, and so on. Now go through each pile in turn, taking care to throw away any specimens which have been damaged, or which you don't want to keep. The ones that are left can now be made ready for pressing.

THE FLOWER PRESS

If you are lucky enough, you may be able to persuade your parents, or your favourite uncle, to buy you a flower press for your birthday. It will look something like this.

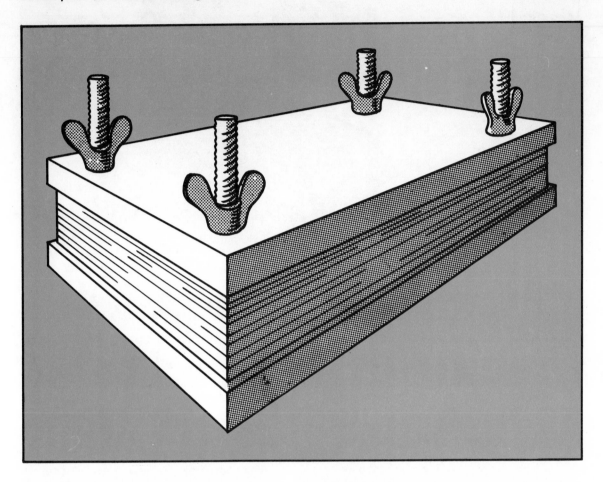

The top and bottom will be of wood, with holes drilled at each corner through which the fastening screws are placed. The nuts used for tightening are called butterfly-nuts. You can guess why, can't you?

Inside the press will be sheets of blotting-paper for pressing the flowers and sheets of cardboard to separate each layer of pressed flowers.

If you are clever with your hands, you can make a flower press for yourself.

You will need:

☞ 2 pieces of wood (plywood will do, about 1 cm thick, each piece being at least 15 cm by 20 cm, with a hole drilled through all four corners).

☞ 4 butterfly-nuts and screws about 6 cm to 10 cm long. Buy the screws before you drill the holes in the wood, to be sure of drilling the right size of hole.

☞ Sheets of pressing paper (newspaper will do).

☞ Sheets of card or corrugated cardboard.

13

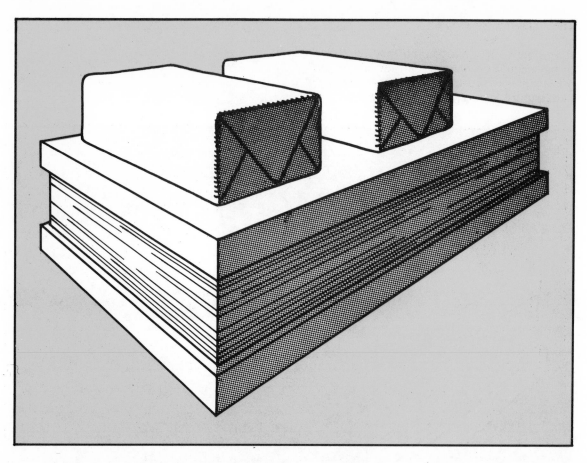

If you can't buy or make a press for yourself — don't worry, you can press your specimens just as well with a press like this.

All you need are two boards, the paper for pressing, and a heavy weight.

This one has two pieces of plywood about 25 cm by 30 cm, and two ordinary house bricks to press the boards together, but any other heavy objects would do just as well. If you use house bricks, wrap them up in brown paper.

THE PRESSING PAPER

Clean blotting-paper is best, but if you can't afford it, almost any other kind of paper will do; the softer and more absorbent it is, the better.

Lining-paper, which you can buy from wallpaper shops, is very good; but failing that, even newspaper can be used, although sometimes the print on the newspaper will leave its mark on the pressed flowers.

You will also need some sheets of cardboard. These you can cut for yourself from old cardboard boxes.

Now you can start to put your flowers into the press.

PRESSING YOUR FLOWERS

Begin with the small, thin leaves and flowers. These should be arranged on the paper like this.

Don't put them too near the edge. Don't let them touch each other. Keep a separate sheet of paper for each different kind of specimen, and make a little paper marker to slip between the two sheets of pressing paper to remind you what the specimens are. If you don't know the name of the specimen, draw a little picture of it — like this.

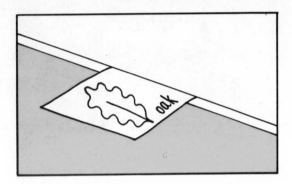

As each sheet is filled, cover it with another sheet of pressing paper, then a piece of cardboard. Place it very carefully in the press and carry on with the next sheet. When all the small specimens have been pressed, begin with the sprays, stalks, grasses and ferns. Remember that when the specimen is completely pressed and dry, its shape cannot be altered, so take care to position the specimens in the shape in which you want them to dry out.

Last of all, the flower-heads with lots of petals — the roses, carnations and Michaelmas daisies. These are too big to press in one piece, so carefully pull off each petal and press it separately. The stem which is left can be thrown away. When all is finished, and you have replaced the top piece of wood and tightened the screws, your press will look like this.

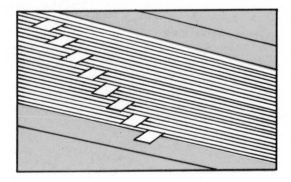

DRYING

The press should now be put away into a dry place (under the stairs, perhaps, in your bedroom, or if there is room, in the airing-cupboard), and left there as long as possible — for at least a week, and if you can bear the suspense, for about four to eight weeks. Some people say that you should change the pressing paper after twenty-four hours to prevent the risk of mildew; but if you are sure that the specimens are quite dry before you press them, this need not be done.

Will you be able to wait for eight weeks? Can you bear the suspense? If not, there is another method of pressing which will allow you to use your dried flowers within about twenty-four hours.

This is what to do.

Arrange your specimens on the pressing paper in exactly the same way as before, putting in your marker and covering it with a second sheet of paper. But, before putting it into the press, iron the whole sheet with a hot iron for about five to ten minutes. (The temperature dial on the iron should be set to WOOL.)

Your mother, or an older brother or sister, will show you how to do this, but be very careful when you come to do it yourself, and never use the iron without your parents' permission.

When all the sheets have been ironed, put them away into the press as before. Leave the press in a warm place for about twenty-four hours, and your specimens will be ready to use.

DESIGNING YOUR PICTURE

Now you can begin to make your first pressed flower picture. This is what you will need:

1. Somewhere quiet to work, and a table to work on. The table should be well lit, so put it near the window or use a table-lamp; and most important of all, there should be no draughts. At this stage, even a sneeze will send your dried petals dancing round the room.

2. Newspaper to cover your working space.

3. A piece of thick coloured paper or card about 20 cm square on which to make your picture.

4. A sharp pencil and ruler.

5. A small jar or tube of Copydex.

6. Some matchsticks (used ones).

And, of course, your flower press. Now wash your hands and you can begin.

You won't need to use all your dried specimens for this first picture, so look carefully at the markers which tell you what you have pressed, and choose two or three sheets of specimens which you think will match the colour of your card. Usually, dark flowers and leaves look better on a light colour; light ones look best on dark.

To help you with the picture, draw in the guidelines which you see here, very faintly in pencil.

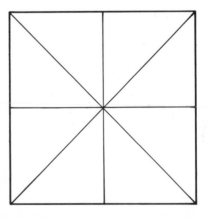

Now choose one of your sheets of specimens and place one specimen on each line, about 2 to 3 cm from the edge of the card, like this.

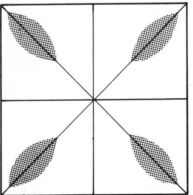

How does it look?

If it looks right, fasten the specimens down. If not, try a different shape or colour of specimen until you are satisfied.

To fasten the specimens down, dip a matchstick into the Copydex, put a very, very tiny blob of it on to the specimen, and gently press the specimen on to the card. That's all. Now fasten down the others.

Next, choose some different kinds of leaves or flowers, and try them out by placing them near the centre of the design — like this.

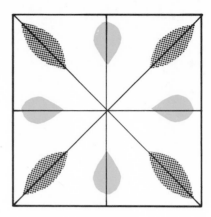

If you think it looks right, fasten them down with tiny blobs of Copydex. If not, try something else.

Last of all, the centre. For this picture, we are going to use four small ivy leaves to make a little star. It looks like this.

There are lots more ways of designing
your picture. Here are some simple ones
to try out first. It will help you if you draw
the guidelines very faintly in pencil.

Here are some other ways, using different sizes and shapes of paper. For a very special picture, you could fasten down your dried specimens on to cloth or felt, and then fix this to a piece of thick cardboard.

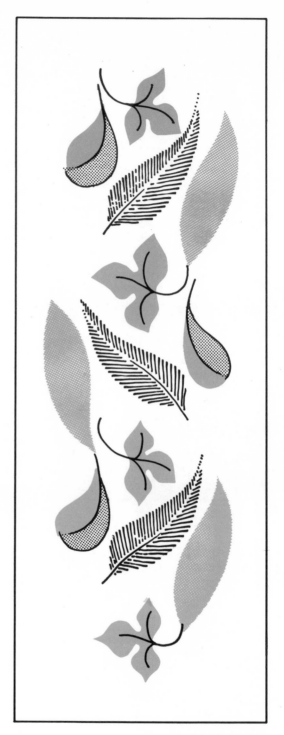

FRAMING YOUR PICTURE

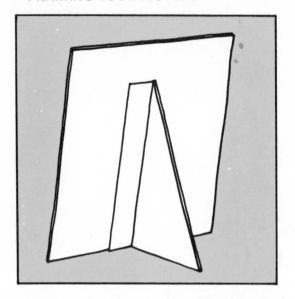

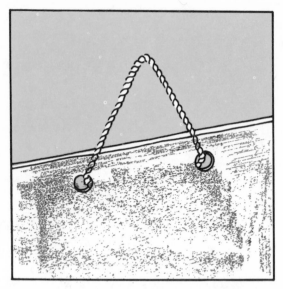

To complete your pressed flower picture you will need to put it into a frame.

For the simplest kind of frame, you will need a piece of stiff cardboard for the back, and a sheet of glass or transparent plastic (both cut to the same size as your picture), and a roll of coloured tape.

Put the backing cardboard, the picture, and the plastic together, and tape very carefully around the edges.

If you want to stand your picture on a table, make a little cardboard support like this, and fasten it on to the back with strong glue.

If you want to hang it on the wall, make two holes in the backing cardboard (before you tape around the edges), and make a hanging loop like this.

Some pictures will look better still if you use a cardboard surround.

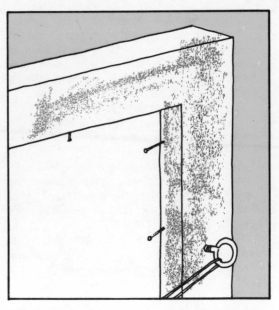

Lastly, you might be able to find an old picture-frame. This will look best of all.

You will need to cut the backing cardboard and the surround to the size of the inside of the frame, and the glass should be cut to the same dimensions. Fasten them together with tape, as before, and hold them firmly in place in the frame with panel pins.

To hang your picture, you will need to screw two eye-hooks into the back of the frame, and thread them with wire or strong string.

OTHER IDEAS FOR PICTURE MAKING

Whenever you want to make a rather special picture for your friend's birthday, or for your parents, it would be a good idea to look around and see whether you can find any interesting flower and leaf designs on the things which you use every day.

If you look carefully, you will find floral designs everywhere. On carpets, wall-papers, curtains, dresses, scarves, ties, even on plates and teapots.

Some of them may seem rather complicated at first, but if you make a sketch in pencil, putting in just the main leaves and flowers, you will be able to use it as an idea for your next picture.

Here are some designs which I have collected. Do you think that any of them could be made into flower pictures?

Keep a sketch-book for yourself, and whenever you see an interesting design — jot it down. Very soon, you should have lots of new ideas.

If you are not very good at drawing, cut out any pictures of flowers and leaves and floral designs which you see in newspapers and magazines, or make tracings of interesting designs from books, to fill an 'ideas' scrapbook.

Collect old seed packets and gardening catalogues. Look at books on art and botany; for these sometimes suggest the best ideas of all.

This picture comes from a very old book called *The General History of Plants*, printed in 1597. Do you think it would make a good flower picture?

If you enjoy making up ideas out of your head, you can try to make an animal picture — or a bird, a fish, or a face picture.

To make a face picture, take out your dried specimens and try to imagine how the different shapes and sizes could be used to make a face. You will need to find two eye-shaped leaves for the eyes, a nose-shaped leaf for the nose, ear-shaped leaves for the ears, and so on. Try out lots of different shapes to begin with, without fastening them down. You can move them about on your backing card with a dry paint-brush or a milk straw with a flattened end.

When you are satisfied with the arrangement, fasten the specimens down with Copydex.

Some more ideas are shown on the following pages. Can you think of any others? Why not try to design a machine, an aeroplane, an elephant, or a palace — an insect, a space creature, a new kind of flower, or even a whole zoo of animals?

Sometimes, you might like to add other kinds of material to your picture.

Can you cut a pattern from a folded sheet of paper, like this?

If you use coloured sticky paper, you can fasten it down on to a piece of card and arrange your pressed leaves and flowers around it and over it, like this.

Or you could cut out a vase-shaped piece of wallpaper, and use your dried specimens to make a vase of flowers.

For this one, I have used a paper doily.
Your mother should be able to find one
for you in the kitchen.

Sometimes, after a busy spell of picture-making, you may find that all your best leaves and flowers have been used up, and all you have left are the very large leaves, and lots of tiny ones.

Don't throw them away.

The large leaves can be used for cutting-up into new shapes. It's quite easy to do with a pair of scissors. See how many different shapes you can make, and see what happens when you put them together.

Some of your cut-down leaves can be used to make a new kind of tree or plant. Draw or paint the stem and branches (felt pens are very good for this), leaving lots of space between them. Now fill in the spaces with your new shapes, as I have done on the opposite page.

Can you think of any other ways of using cut leaves?

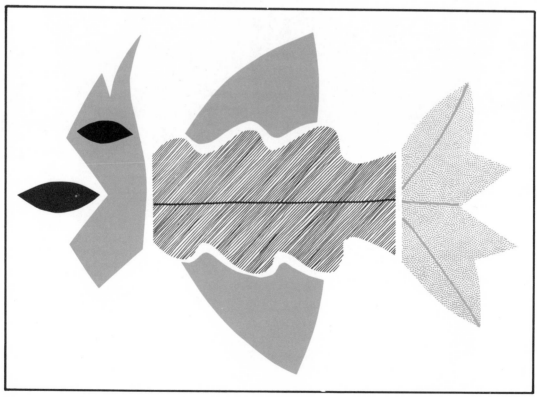

With lots of small leaves or petals, all of the same shape and size, you can make a pattern picture. Before you begin, draw these lines on your paper. See how many different ways you can arrange your specimens.

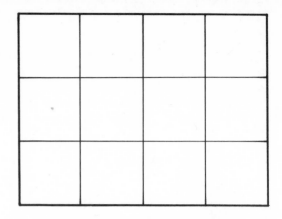

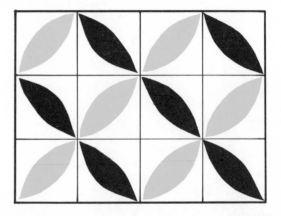

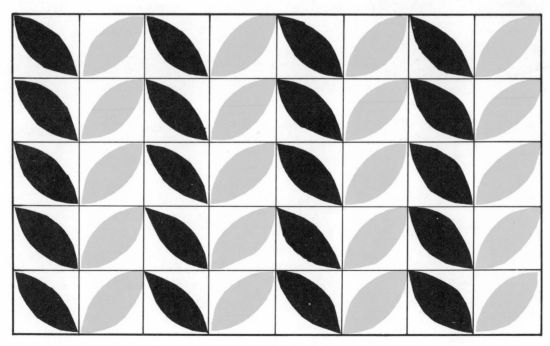

Last of all, you could make an 'initial' picture. This is a very personal kind of picture which you can make for yourself, or for your best friend, using the first letter of the Christian name as a shape to decorate with leaves and flowers.

You can see pictures of decorated initial letters in very old books, where the first letter of each new chapter is made to look something like this one. It comes from a book once owned by King Charles II.

To make your own initial picture, draw the shape of the initial you want to use, in pencil, colouring in the shape with crayon or felt pen. Now use your leaves and flowers to make a pattern around it.

Like this.

OTHER THINGS TO MAKE

Now for some other articles to make with your pressed leaves and flowers.

CHRISTMAS CARDS

Christmas is an expensive time for everybody, and there never seems to be enough pocket-money to buy all the presents and cards which you want to give to your friends.

Next Christmas, why not save some of your pocket-money by making your own flower-picture cards?

This is what to do.

1. Buy the envelopes for the cards first (the cheap, brown ones will do), so that you can cut the card to the right size. If you do it the other way round, it may be difficult to find an envelope which fits the card.

2. Next you will need some sheets of card. Any colour will do, but red might be best. You will be able to buy the card at your local art shop.

3. Now cut the large sheets of card into smaller sizes which fit neatly into the envelopes.

Don't forget to cut the card slightly smaller than the envelope size, and don't forget that your card will be folded. If the envelope is 15 cm by 10 cm, your card should be 14 cm by 18 cm. When folded in two, it becomes 14 cm by 9 cm; just the right size to fit into the envelope.

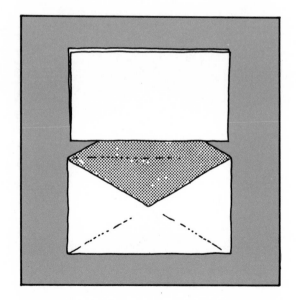

4. Now for your design.

You can use any kinds of leaves and flowers, even those which you collected in the summer, but it might be a better idea to use something Christmassy.

If all your specimens have been used up, you can collect some more and press them quickly, as I showed you on page 16. Even in December you can still find lots of leaves and flowers about. Chickweed remains green in the coldest months, and even if you can't find a late rose or Michael-mas daisy, there will still be tiny rock flowers, evergreens and grasses. Best of all, use the leaves that we associate with Christmas: mistletoe and ivy, spruce and fir. You can use holly leaves too, but you might find them rather hard to press flat.

BIRTHDAY CARDS AND VALENTINES

For a birthday card or a Valentine, make it extra special by using your friend's favourite flower. Better still, you can send your friend a message by using the language of flowers. Everybody knows that red roses are for love, but do you know what a daisy means, or a tulip?

Here are some of the flowers and leaves which you might like to use, and their meanings:

Beech	*Prosperity*
Daisy	*Innocence*
Elm	*Dignity*
Fern	*Fascination*
Hawthorn	*Hope*
Ivy	*Marriage*
Larch	*Boldness*
Mint	*Virtue*
Oak	*Bravery*
Parsley	*Festivity*
Pear	*Affection*
Peony	*Bashfulness*
Snowdrop	*Hope*
Strawberry	*Love*
Sycamore	*Curiosity*
Tulip	*Fame*

Here are some that you should think twice about using!

Anemone	*Sickness*
Harebell	*Grief*
Lavender	*Distrust*
Sweet Pea	*Departure*
Raspberry	*Sadness*
Rhododendron	*Danger*

And worst of all, the wild tansy. It means, *I declare war against you.*

BOOK COVERS

This would be a good way of decorating some of your favourite books.

1. Cover the book with plain, coloured paper.

2. Fasten a design of leaves and flowers on to the paper cover.

3. Cover the finished book with a transparent, adhesive plastic, like Transpaseal.

Now your book will last longer, and look much more attractive.

A BOOKMARK

Make a flower design on a piece of card about 15 cm by 5 cm, and cover it with transparent, adhesive plastic. If you want to, you can add a short tassel of wool, like this.

A SET OF TABLE MATS

You will need:

☞ Thick cardboard or pieces of hardboard, for the base.

☞ Sheets of transparent plastic, or a roll of adhesive plastic to cover the flower pictures.

☞ Some coloured, adhesive tape.

1. Cut up your cardboard or hardboard into six pieces, each one about 15 cm square. If you use hardboard, get someone to help you with the cutting, and sandpaper the edges.

2. Cut six pieces of thin card or paper. These should be the same size as the bases, and will be used for your flower pictures.

3. Design your pictures and fasten them down on to the paper.

4. Fasten the finished designs on to the cardboard or hardboard bases with Copydex.

5. Cover the design with a sheet of thin plastic (cut to the same size as the base), and tape very carefully around the edges, so that the base and plastic are held firmly together. If you use adhesive plastic, cut a piece about 3 or 4 cm bigger than the base all the way round, and fold the overhanging edges of the plastic underneath the base.

   To make your mats even better, fasten a piece of felt or fabric on to the back of the base with Copydex.

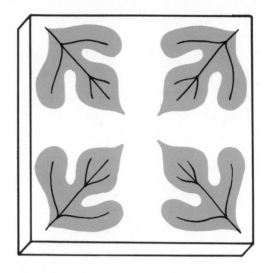

DOOR-PLATES

Door-plates are used on doors, placed just above the doorknob, to prevent the dirty marks which people make when pushing open the door with their hand.

If your house doesn't have them, you might persuade your mother to let you make one for your own bedroom door. Later on, perhaps, when your mother sees how useful it is, she might ask you to make one for each of the doors in the house.

Transparent plastic door-plates can be bought from hardware shops. They look like this, with a hole at top and bottom for screwing the plate on to the door.

To make your plate picture, cut out a piece of card, the same shape and size as the plate. Design your picture and fasten it down on to the card. Put the card and the plate together and screw them to the door.

OTHER THINGS TO DO

MAKING RUBBINGS

For this, you will need some thin, white paper and a box of coloured wax crayons.

Look through your specimens and choose those which have rough surfaces and ridged veins.

Now take a rubbing of your specimen by covering it with a sheet of thin, white paper; and gently but firmly rub over the top with one of your wax crayons.

Here are some leaf rubbings.

If you make lots of them in different colours, you can cut them out and use them to make a rubbing picture like this one.

Fasten them on to card with Polycell or flour-and-water paste.

MAKING SPLATTER AND STENCIL PICTURES

For this you will need some poster paints, a stiff brush and an old toothbrush.

To make a stencil print, stipple around the edge of a leaf with the stiff brush. Use the paint fairly thickly, but apply only a little of it to the end of your brush. If you use too much, it will smudge and blot.

To make a splatter print, dip your old toothbrush into thick paint, point the brush downwards over the leaf, and splatter the paint around the edge of the leaf by drawing back the bristles with a stiff piece of card, or an old kitchen knife.

With practice, you will be able to make a splatter and stencil picture using lots of different shapes and colours.

MAKING A LOOK-THROUGH PICTURE

Instead of fastening down your pressed leaves and flowers on to paper, fasten them down on to a piece of transparent cellophane or plastic. You can use Copydex for fastening the specimens to the cellophane but the white of an egg is best. Perhaps your mother will let you have some. When your picture is finished, cover it with a sheet of transparent, adhesive plastic, and bind the edges together with adhesive tape.

Make two holes in the top of the picture; thread them with cotton, and hang your picture in front of a window.

FINDING OUT ABOUT LEAVES AND FLOWERS

If you want to find out more about the specimens which you have collected — what they are called, when they flower, where they grow, and so on — it would be a good idea to keep some of them in a special 'finding-out' book.

Your collection can be made up of any of the leaves and flowers which you have pressed, but it's more fun, and you will find out more, by limiting the kinds of specimen which you collect.

It could be:

An alphabet collection — where you try to find a flower, leaf or plant whose name begins with each letter of the alphabet. Ds and Bs will be quite easy, for you could choose a daisy, dandelion, dahlia or daffodil; a bay-leaf, bindweed, birch, blue-bell or buttercup, and so on. But what about something beginning with K, Q, U or Z? You may have to wait a long time before you find a kingcup, quaking grass, or ulex. Something for Z you must find out for yourself.

A garden collection — where you make a pressing of all the flowers in your garden.

A colour collection — where you collect only the plants which have a certain colour of flower. . . blue, white, yellow, or red.

A favourite collection — of your very favourite flowers and leaves.

A shape collection — where each page is used for leaves and petals of a certain shape.

A walk-to-school collection — of flowers and leaves which you find on your way to school.

A spring collection — of the plants which flower in the spring. You could make one for winter, summer, and autumn too.

When you have decided what to collect, you will need something to keep your collection in. You can use an exercise book, or a drawing-book, with plain, white pages, or you could mount your specimens on pieces of card, and keep them together in a paper wallet.

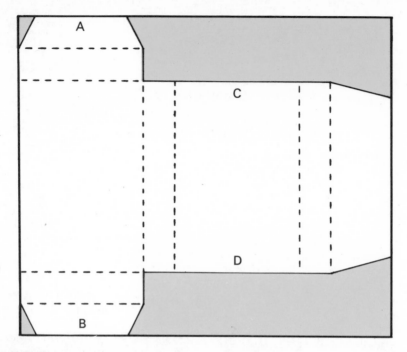

If you decide to use a wallet, you will be able to buy one from a stationer's — or (to save your pocket-money) make one for yourself.

You will need a sheet of thick paper or manila (a kind of thinnish card), about 50 cm by 60 cm.

Draw in these lines very carefully; cut away all the shaded parts, and fold along the dotted lines. Fasten A to C, and B to D, with Copydex.

The finished folder will look like this.

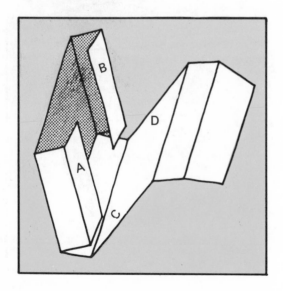

For the mounting sheets, use white paper or card.

When you have collected your specimens, press and dry them, and fasten them into your book, or on to your mounting cards with Copydex (as if you were making a picture). Don't use sticky tape, or the pages will stick together.

Sometimes you might press the whole plant, like this.

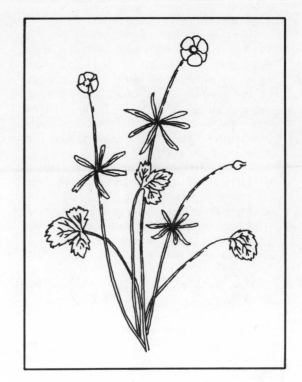

If you want to learn more about the different parts of the plant, you might press the parts down separately, like this.

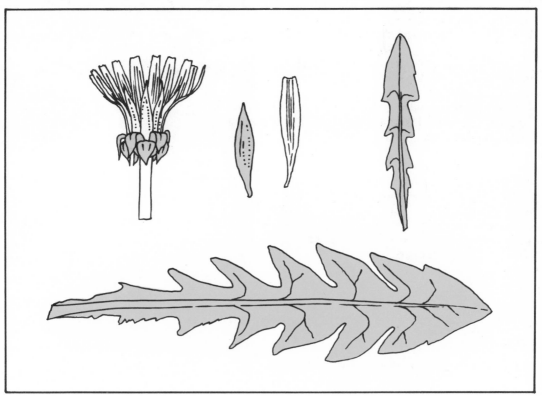

THINGS TO WRITE ABOUT

1. The name of the plant. All plants have more than one name. Some plants are called by different names in different parts of the country. A bluebell, for instance, might also be called a bell bottle — blue trumpets — or fairy bells. You can guess why, can't you? These are rather like nicknames. But it also has a scientific name — *Endymion nonscriptus*. It's a difficult name to pronounce, and even more difficult to remember, but it's useful if you ever talk to a Chinaman. He wouldn't know what you meant by 'bluebell' but scientists all over the world would know what an *Endymion nonscriptus* is.

2. The day when you picked it. Just put the date: *3 May 1974* — or — *3.5.74*.

3. Where you found it. Draw a little map.

4. What other kinds of plants were growing nearby.

5. The colour of it. Don't forget that after pressing and drying, the colour will change.

6. Last of all, write down anything else which you can find out about it.

It's easy to guess why a daisy is called a daisy — because it's the day's eye. The dandelion has a French name, 'dent de lion', which means 'tooth of the lion'. Can you think why? And why is it unlucky to bring hawthorn blossom into the house?

Can you find out how your plants got their names?

To help you with all this, try to persuade your parents to buy you an identification book of flowers and trees.

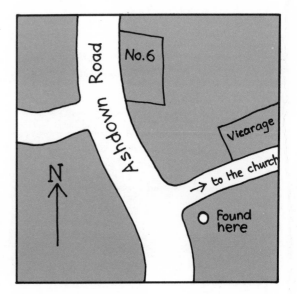